Fight
Flight

Psychology

ISBN 978-91-7699-806-9

Förlag: BoD – Books on Demand, Stockholm, Sverige
Tryck: BoD – Books on Demand, Norderstedt, Tyskland

Illustrations, graphical form, composition and cover illustration: Staffan Garpebring.

Translated into English by Joseph Sinnott in consultation with Staffan Garpebring, author of the original title Stressreflexer och Tankefällor (2008)

Thanks to Joe for his linguistic sensitivity and creativity in the translation of this text.

Foreword

In this book I have revised and extended the contents of my book *Stress Reflexes reflecting and affecting Perception of Life* to give additional information to psychotherapists and clients about my theoretical frame of reference and my practice with clients. I wrote the swedish original *Stressreflexer och tankefällor* to help clients get a better understanding of fight-flight responses and their impact on our self-esteem, our mental, emotional and behavioural habits, and their consequences on our mental and physical health.

I believe that if we wish to comprehend the complex nature of life, we will fail if we disregard a systemic approach. A systemic psychological frame of reference ("FRAMES") that is presented in this book was developed in my work at a youth centre in cooperation with my young clients.

Fight flight reflexes, calming reflexes and the feeling of gratification influence our sensual and mental focus, our emotion and action. Interaction between bodily and psychological function forms a "figure-ground" perception of our world, our life and our "self". I.e. some phenomena come to the fore whilst others are put in the background.

Over and over again I will revert to six psychological components: Sensory focus, reaction in the body, action, mental reflection/focus, emotion and how we perceive ourselves as a whole (as a complete sensual human being).

Thereby I wish to contribute to the understanding of stress, anxiety and depression.

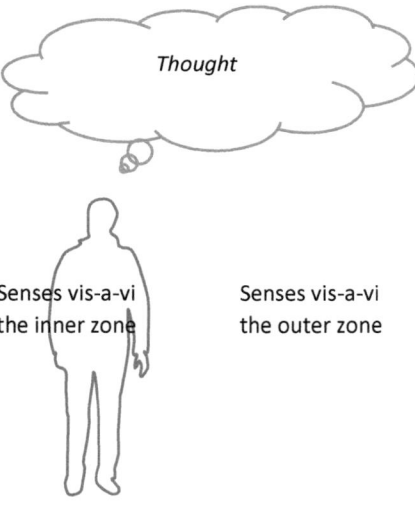

In the thought zone we process thoughts and concepts. We receive sensory input from the outer zone through our five senses; sight, hearing, smell, taste and touch. Sensory input from the body comes through our inner senses; sense of balance, muscle sense (which informs the brain about our movements, and how tense muscles are), and many other nerve receptors which report to the brain when we are hungry, thirsty, in pain, if we are hot or cold, anxious or relaxed, etc.

In mindfulness, i.e. acceptance of the here and now, we scan the three zones without getting stuck in any of them. This way we can be more in contact with our needs and emotions, and the present situation, instead of fleeing mentally or thinking aggressively. Thereby we can also communicate better with other people.

FRAMES is an abbreviation of the following components of our psyché:

Formation of outer sensory input ("shaping/placing together" impressions from sight, hearing, smell, taste and touch).

   And formation of inner sensations *from inside the body* due to thought, memories and associations, or due to outer sensory input – **Sensory attention.**

Reactions; (reflexes) in the body.

Physiological reactions, stress, relaxation, satisfaction, physical balance or imbalance.

Action; behaviour, body language and facial expressions. Linguistic expressions

Mental reflection; processing memories of previous relations and thought of upcoming relations. Cognitive function

Emotion; indignation, excitement, happiness, sedition, discomfort etc.

Self experience; self-image, self esteem, self confidence

Contents

Introduction

Imagine that you are walking down the street and you see that you are about to meet a group of loud youths. Your reactions to this situation can be different depending on what emotional state you are in at that given moment in time and experiences in similar situations. You may think about how you would behave if you were in such a group talking about music, the latest film you have seen, or just chatting about anything at all. However, if you are having a bad day or you have previously felt out of place in a similar situation you may feel stressed by the presence of these youths.

Many clients that I meet in therapy sessions at the Youth Centre recognize the following scenario: "When I see the youths I get butterflies in my stomach, my heart starts to palpitate, I tense up, start fidgeting with my coat, bag or mobile phone, become self-conscious of how I walk, start to feel nervous and experience lower self-esteem." This description of a personal experience can be analyzed using the FRAMES model which is a check list I use when I meet clients afflicted by inner stress. The causes of inner stress vary and can manifest themselves in many different ways.

We can analyze the situation above in the following way using the **FRAMES** model:

F - Focus of attention: See and hear the youths.

R - Reaction within the body: Butterflies, stiffer, tenser gait and palpitations.

A - Action: Start to fidget with my coat, mobile phone etc.

M - Mental focus: Become self-conscious of how I walk.

E - Emotional reaction: Feel nervous and anxious.

S – Self esteem: Is affected negatively.

Inner stress can encompass everything from stimulating, possibly exaggerated interest in something you have a passion for, irritation, an uncomfortable feeling of restlessness to an unbearable, horrifying feeling of panic and angst. No matter how we react to it, stress affects the way we live our lives.

In my work as a psychologist I am struck by the fact that clients who come to me with emotional and social problems often do not know much about the relationship between their thoughts and their reactions to stress and how fight-flight reflexes in the body actually contribute to their psychological problems.

When we perceive a possible threat we develop "tunnel vision" and filter what we hear. This is an inevitable consequence of the physiological changes that occur when the body prepares for "fight-flight". Sensory impressions are amplified automatically as our bodies mobilize in preparation for what may happen. We prepare for potentially threatening situations that could arise, and if nothing happens we start to think; "what if ….?" – and an anguish evoking state of alert may arise.

In this book I wish to emphasize the importance of bodily reactions in the analysis of psychological problems. The body's reaction to stress affects our psychosomatic circuit fundamentally.

Changes occur in the body including the executive centre of the body – in other words, the brain.

Chapter 1. Life is in the body

The new-born baby clearly experiences life through its body, in the present. When the baby is content its body is totally at ease. When it is hungry it fumbles after its mother's breast, starts to whine and eventually, if it does not find nourishment, starts to cry. When the baby needs to expel bodily waste, it just does it, without a sense of shame. When the baby wants company, it cries out for attention and so on. – A state of utopia you might think, before the child becomes aware of "the tree of know-ledge". The experiences of our formative years create "the child within".

Childhood memories reflect the growing ability to handle relationships with others and deal with everyday life. The growing intellectual skills of the "child within" are inter-twined with physical memories i.e. memories of bodily reactions to different experiences in life. The consequences of the child's actions, in different situations, form its way of dealing with difficulties i.e. "coping strategies". Adjusting, being aggressive, creative, invisible, a clown, good or caring are all different behaviours the child may develop.

In any given situation the child will use the behaviour that is best rewarded. Usually the child chooses the behaviour that gives it the most physical satisfaction. The resultant positive feelings reinforce the child's propensity to adopt that particular behaviour in the future and in time the behaviour becomes automatic. In other words, the child's behavioural response to different situations becomes more and more subconscious.

If an adult behaves in the same way as a little child, acting on its immediate needs (Oh! An ice cream van – I want ice cream – NOW!!) he/she may be perceived as spontaneous and charming or spoilt. If an adult shows a lot of egocentric, childish traits, he/she is seen as rowdy and irritating by other adults.

Over years we learn different ways to deal with and control our immediate bodily responses. We sometimes repress inner images and thoughts that trigger bodily responses in order to hide these responses. We can overcompensate and act even more politely towards someone when we are scared of or angry at that person. We can master our bodily urges and concentrate totally on one thing or on another person's wishes.

When we meditate, however, everything is allowed to come and go and we can experience happy or sorrowful physical memories or bring to mind troublesome episodes. Thoughts, memories, fears, sorrows, things that make us happy or unhappy or any bodily phenomena are all parts of the self and should therefore be accepted and acknowledged by us.

Good meditation does not allow us to get bogged down in psychological or bodily phenomena.

Instead it acknowledges the "self" in its fullness; experiences, wisdom and creativity.

Our breathing reflects how we feel inside and is, in itself, an experience of being. Every time we see in "tunnel vision" and lose ourselves in troublesome thought – thereby losing contact with the self as a whole – we can achieve mindfulness or become consciously aware of our current situation by concentrating on our breathing.

The figure below represents a way of seeing oneness of being. It shows five parts of the self – The figure in the middle represents the self.

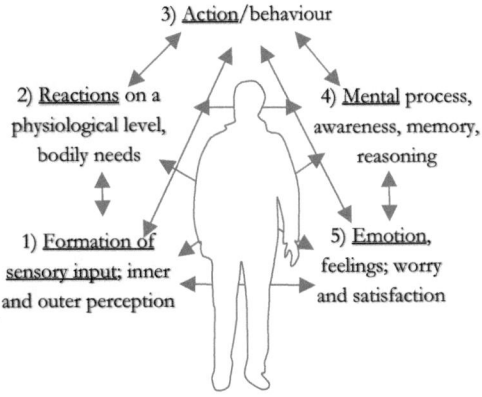

3) Action/behaviour

2) Reactions on a physiological level, bodily needs

4) Mental process, awareness, memory, reasoning

1) Formation of sensory input; inner and outer perception

5) Emotion, feelings; worry and satisfaction

Psychological phenomena have been described in many different ways throughout the ages and there is an enormous amount of information about them available nowadays. In my practice with clients I realised I needed a reasonably simple model to show the complex systemic interaction between body and mind. Therefore I conceived the FRAMES model.

Chapter 2.   The **FRAMES** model

The **FRAMES** model encompasses emotions, thoughts, actions and conceptions of self. But above all I have chosen to highlight physiological phenomena and selective perception, i.e. shaping or compiling sensory impressions so that they make sense and have meaning.   Last but not least, I wanted to find a model to address a particular phenomenon to be analysed – systemic circularity. The question; "which came first – the chicken or the egg?" represents that central quandary in all studies of biological cyclical systems. The human psyche is a cyclical system.

There are numerous mutual relations between different aspects of the psyche and the body. For example, do I get a certain feeling because I think of a particular thing? Or, do I think about a particular thing because I have a certain feeling?

The relationship between mind and body works both ways. Interactions within the **FRAMES** model are reciprocal – every aspect of the **FRAMES** model mutually affects every other aspect of the model. Our senses focus on and constantly relay impressions to our brain. We are taught that we have five senses but that is an understatement. Hearing, vision, smell, taste and touch are five senses but we also have balance and kinaesthetic sense. Touch comprises several different sensory impressions; heat, cold, pressure, the feeling of gentle touch or

19

the experience of pressure deeper inside the body. Inside the body nerve cells relay information to the brain about pain, breathing, heart palpitations, excitement. We can comprehend when we are hungry, thirsty, tired, need to go to the toilet etc.

There is an awful amount of sensations being relayed to the brain. Impressions communicated through our senses can be external (from the zone outside our bodies) or internal (from inside the body). When we focus our attention on something, it is often done subconsciously.

Mindfulness involves awareness of what we are paying attention to, and allowing sensory impressions the same importance as our thoughts. "Lose your mind and come to your senses" is a witty pun used to describe the importance of being aware of what our senses relate to us.

In our civilization intellect is often favoured. Experiences of perception (sensualism) are, at the most, something we ponder on in our spare time. However, sensualism during working hours could probably prevent us from being burnt-out, from feeling irritation and dissatisfaction at work.

In order to be aware of and prevent symptoms of stress we must be sensually, as well as mentally, conscious of them. How do I feel physically? What is the reason for feeling this way? Am I currently thinking about something that is stressing me? – We need to respect our breaks.

If we, due to sensual unawareness, do not notice physical stress until it is at a very high level, we are at risk of developing tunnel vision by the time we actually recognize the symptoms of inner stress. I may then feel very ill at ease and wonder if there is something wrong with my heart for example. Can the pain I have in my neck be caused by cancer?

The limitation of our attention span that occurs when we are worried or nervous makes it more difficult to think rationally and we get entangled in the details. Even when our fear is only a "false alarm", and there is no real danger, we easily disregard observations that indicate that there is no danger.

Mind traps are built on selective (filtered) focusing on threats due to the stress reflex. Our focus on sensory impressions occurs more or less consciously and is concentrated on whatever interests us the most. Sometimes we are completely unaware of why we focus on a particular thing.

When I am worried I look for things that worry me. It is like looking through binoculars, we may see in great details but we miss the greater perspective. Instead we easily *construct* a *whole* picture, of what we think it is.

This is the essence of projection. We can project inner thoughts and emotions onto other people and the surrounding situation because we do not know all the facts and we fill in missing pieces in the puzzle.

21

When we think, we pick out and process impressions from inside or outside our bodies. If I am walking down the street and I am really hungry, my thoughts will be pre-occupied with food and I will be inclined to notice all the grocery stores, restaurants, pubs and fastfood stands. If I am really cold I will only have eyes for places that are warm. When I want new clothes, I look for clothes stores.

If we are worried and adopt a defensive attitude we will be inclined to anticipate hostility and foul intentions in the actions of others whether they are true or just a figment of our imaginations.

Worry, irritability or other reactions are regulated by the autonomic nervous system which even controls palpitations, breathing as well as the constriction and dilation of blood-vessels. Tingling and numbness in your arms and legs or a headache can all be caused by reflexes in the autonomic nervous system.

What is a feeling, an emotion? We can feel happy, tired, melancholic, mad, disappointed, hungry, contented etc. We use countless words for feelings and each word has a special meaning. However, people do not necessarily agree on what words that describe feelings mean for them.

This is due to the fact that people have different associations or experiences attached to words that describe feelings.

One thing is certain, when we do have feelings they are initialized by reflexes of the nervous system and our physiological responses to them.

Action arises from our focus of attention, our thoughts and our feelings (the way our body responds to sensations or thoughts). Perceptions we have of ourselves, self-esteem and self confidence have developed through interaction between the different facets of FRAMES.

To sum it up: Our experiences can be described in the following components:

(1) Focus-formation in attention towards various outer phenomena and inner, physiological states (selective perception)

(2) Reactions in the body (physiology; hormones etc)

(3) Actions (behaviour, attitude)

(4) Mental conceptions ("mental action")

(5) Emotions and

(6) Self awareness.

Accordingly, we can denote every experience as a FRAME that gradually give rise to self awareness.

Dialectic FRAMES Therapy; a mix of Gestalt Therapy, Cognitive Behaviour Therapy and Systemic Family Therapy, is based on the formula:

O – [FRAMES] – EO

O stands for "Outer situation" including other people's FRAMES. EO stands for effects of FRAMES in the outer situation. A person's behaviour and attitude mutually interact with that person's circumstantial conditions. Dialectic from Greek (dialegein) means take apart. Dialectic FRAMES Therapy means to take apart – to analyze interaction within a person's FRAMES, and between different persons' FRAMES.

A vast majority of FRAMES eventually become automatic due to repetitive learning. Some FRAMES contribute to happiness, joy and pleasure whilst others involve stress, sorrow and anxiety. When arousal in the body is high it can narrow our attention span drastically. Tunnel vision and filtered listening is an essential phenomenon in catastrophic thinking as well as mania.

Chapter 3. Autonomic Reflexes

Reflexes of the autonomic nervous system induce a certain feeling within us and are an important part of our psyche. The central nervous system (the brain and spinal chord) picks up and processes sensory impressions which induce the thought process and corresponding behaviour.

The autonomic nervous system is connected to the central nervous system and plays a role in the relationship between thoughts and feelings. We can be in charge of our focus of attention, our thoughts and actions, whereas feelings are automatic due to autonomic reactions.

If we have a certain feeling it is likely that certain thoughts, that spark this feeling, come to the fore again. "Shall I be so nervous the next time I have to speak publicly?" Or "It is going to be great fun to go to the cinema this evening!"

Psycho-therapy is about to process and develop the relationship between thoughts and feelings so that we become less helpless when confronted with our feelings.

Personal emotions are not always recognized by others or even by ourselves. We have all learned how to suppress our feelings or ignore our needs. When we get angry we are encouraged to stifle our anger etc.

Positive feelings and desire occur when the "pleasure area" of the brain is activated and we feel good. We feel satisfaction when we have eaten our fill. When we are touched, the hormone oxytocin is released which makes us feel good.

But the inherent relaxation response may become weaker after years of inner stress and insufficient relaxation. Social interaction teaches us not to let desire or lack of desire control our behaviour. But if we do not allow our feelings to influence us then we risk psychosomatic stress symptoms.

At the same time, if we do not allow common sense and rational thought to reign over our feelings we may do stubborn or stupid things that may result in an inner stress.

In this book I intend to show that the fight-flight response (mobilization of energy due to a stressor), besides being a major exertion, can be a health hazard, especially over extended periods of time, if there is no time for psycho-somatic recovery.

For your own sake, it is good advice not to get too excited about the red light at the traffic lights. If you notice that you have a tendency to get worked up about insignificant things you should see it as a sign of inner stress that needs to be tackled.

Stress reflexes can be upsetting even when we are not actually conscious of what triggers them off. The following short excerpt will help illustrate my point. It is from the journal of a young man,

Michael, who contacted me for help with anxiety and restlessness.

At the previous session we talked about inner stress, fightflight reaction and anxiety evoking anticipation. Michael has noticed that he becomes anxious when driving his car on his way to work. He wants to know why. I explain how thoughts or impressions can lead to stress reactions. I ask him what he thinks about, hears or sees on his way to work.

He cannot think of anything. So I recount how I used to feel stress when I was on my way to a job I had earlier. If something happened in traffic, however trivial, that caught my attention, I could feel a twinging pain in my stomach. This was, of course, unpleasant and I realized it was a stress reflex. The stressful situation I experienced in traffic, although trivial, was "the straw that broke the camels back". The job I had at that time was stressful.

Michael could relate to my story, as he had felt the same way when he went to school. He has dyslexia and when he was in the car, on his way to school, he worried about how his day would be.

He currently has a job that he enjoys, but the route he travels to work is the same as the route he took to school. In other words, Michael was experiencing a learned automated stress reflex coupled to driving along a certain route.

Today he has a job that he likes and he feels competent in his work there. I tell him that the next time he feels this stress reflex on his way to work he should think and say to himself: "Here comes that stress reflex again but now I know why. Things are different now. I am an adult, I know a lot more and I am good at what I do at work. Things are not the same anymore and I can relax and feel calm".

When I tell Michael this a big smile lights up his face. We talk about the FRAMES model where thoughts evoke feelings and feelings remind us of the thoughts we had when we experienced these feelings earlier.

This reminds Michael of several examples of automated stress reflexes that we can analyse in a similar fashion.

You might say that we cannot control stress reflexes since they are autonomous reflexes. But we can control how the body reacts to stress reflexes through relaxation, mindfulness, bio-feedback, lifestyle changes, new ways of thinking, exercise and psycho-therapy.

Chapter 4. Stress Reflexes – Fight-Flight Response

Inherent energy mobilizing reflexes prepare us for fight-flight when danger is at hand. Unfortunately, they also lead to fear, aggression and a multitude of distressing experiences such as; irritation, anguish, depression, phobias, compulsive thinking and action, addictive behaviour, post traumatic stress syndrome, generalized anxiety, paranoia, prejudice and last but not least, conflicts between individuals and groups.

How can we explain what happens when the body mobilizes energy in preparation for fight-flight? The pattern of physiological reactions is, on the whole, the same as that of a cat when it is threatened by an angry dog or that of a zebra that is endangered by a flock of lions.

Imagine a zebra grazing on the savannah. Suddenly it picks up a scent that it associates with chaos and horror. How does the zebra's body react? When the zebra senses the smell of a lion, stress hormones are pumped out into the body and lead to the following effects:

•Senses are heightened. The zebra becomes even more adept at hearing or seeing the lion. The pupils of the eyes dilate, sense of hearing becomes even keener and the zebra listens attentively.

•Muscles contract. The zebra is on its mark, ready to take off at a sprint within a fraction of a second.

•Sugars are released into the blood to supply muscles with fuel for maximum performance.

•The heart beats harder and faster to pump energy; (fuel and oxygen,) to the muscles and to carry away carbon dioxide which is formed when the body burns fuel.

•Breathing frequency and volume increase.

•Digestion ceases.

•The zebra concentrates automatically on the lions and their behaviour.

All these reactions are healthy and functional responses to stress that help the zebra to survive and subsequently spawn offspring that will inherit the same ability to react quickly to a fight-flight situation. The offspring who inherit the best aptitude for fight-flight have the best chances of survival.

However, there is one crucial difference between a zebra and a human being; i.e. our intelligence and ability to think imaginatively.

When the threatening situation has passed we still continue to experience it because we can conjure up a range of similar or even worse scenarios. We can easily envisage the threatening situation reoccurring. Imagine that the lion comes back, or several lions appear, and some from other directions, as well. What would happen if I tripped or if I couldn't run fast enough!

This type of imaginative thinking is not possible in the zebras mind. Unfortunately, the human imagination and stress reflexes subject us to anguish, phobias, compulsive thoughts and eventually depression. Anguish in human beings is actually the result of two valuable capacities and their interaction – the fight-flight response and intelligence.

The hunted zebra reacts directly to the fight-flight situation and goes on as usual after the situation has ended. If the zebra survives it will leave the whole situation behind and go on with its life. Stress levels are reduced to normal. Muscles relax, the heart beats slower, breathing is calmer, blood sugar has been metabolized and digestion can resume. The zebra can now relax again and a state of rest ensues.

More often than not, we do not allow stress reflexes to reign in the same manner as zebras do. In actual fact this is the same as not being allowed to eat when we are hungry, smell good food and begin to salivate and the stomach automatically prepares for food. If the body cannot allow itself to react immediately the mobilized energy and stress remain in the body and it will take a while for it to subside.

Immediate reaction, without room for thought, can be reckless, leading to actions we may later regret. Dealing with this is probably one of our greatest challenges.

Spontaneity can make us feel more alive but acting impulsively can also lead to failure, guilt and shame.

Inner stress that remains in the body for a long time magnifies focus on threatening impressions. All fight-flight behaviours, that can reduce inner stress, have the potential to develop into automated behaviour or obsessive thought.

Usually we strive to escape from inner stress, to avoid fear and aggression. Behaviours and mental attitudes that decrease inner stress or increase relaxation are willingly reinforced, even if they are detrimental in the long run (neglect or denial of stress evoking information, phobic and obsessive behaviour, addiction to dugs or shopping etc.). It is better then to deal directly with the stress reflex.*

(*see Chapter 12; How to handle Mind Traps and Learned Stress Reflexes)

Chapter 5. Prolonged anguish evoking State of Alert

When stress reflexes prevail it can be a very intricate dilemma – on the one hand, to recognise the real dangers and, on the other hand, to recognise when dangers are imaginary (false alarm).

Brooding, i.e. pondering morbidly and persistently, can make us sick. "Mind trap brooding" is detrimental to our health. When we are alone, brooding on problems that we cannot solve, we tend to imagine catastrophic scenarios or possible negative chains of events that may occur.

Those who seek my help usually suffer from inner stress. When I show them the following list of stress reactions that take place due to fight-flight reflexes they often recognize the symptoms as their own reactions:

•Unwillingly focusing on possible threats leads to worrying thoughts being "lodged" in our consciousness and these thoughts "go round and round". When we wake up in the morning, it takes only a few seconds or minutes until we are preoccupied with these thoughts again. During the day they may fade into the background while we are engaged in our daily activities but they resurface when we unwind in the evening. "The threat" may be great or small.

•Our state of alertness makes us oversensitive for aural or visual disturbances, and we find it hard to concentrate. Memory is affected and that in itself is a reason for irritation – stress hormones continue to flow in the body and even affect sleep.

•Increased blood sugar levels can generate fluctuations in sugar levels which in turn lead to energy and mood swings.

•As well as being very sore, tight muscles make us feel tense and awkward.

•Unsettled digestion encompasses "butterflies in the stomach", dryness of mouth, loss of appetite, nausea, intestinal dysfunction and stomach pain.

•Palpitations are disturbing (can be scary) and increase blood pressure.

•Faster breathing can lead to hyperventilation (rapid chest breathing) and a feeling of uneasy breathing. You feel short of breath even though you actually breathe too fast. You feel dizzy.

Feeling anguish can rub off on most experiences. Stress reflexes are activated in a growing amount of situations and are linked to more and more conditions; anguish becomes more generalized. This depletes the body's resources. In the long run the body cannot handle it and this may eventually lead to depression.

One of the most evident signs of depression is when, during a prolonged period of time, things that used to be great fun feel pointless and hollow.

Living with worry and anguish affects the whole FRAMES system; focus of attention, reactions within the body, action, mental conception, emotions and self-esteem.

Focus of attention and sensory alertness is affected by the mobilization of energy that occurs when we experience a fight-flight situation. The heightened senses render us easily disturbed and vexed. In the end the brain cannot take in any more information.

Bodily reactions; dryness of mouth, stomach pain, palpitations, elevated blood pressure, breathing difficulties with pins and needles in the skin, dizziness, sore and tense muscles, elevated blood sugar levels can all manifest themselves to varying degrees. These symptoms are very unpleasant and of course very difficult to live with.

Elevated stress levels affect our actions. We begin to avoid certain situations or become excessively aggressive, reacting too strongly to situations that normally should not lead to aggressive behaviour.

This can lead to "setback consequences". Our behaviour is counter productive and only affects ourselves adversely. Dysfunctional actions due to inner stress can appear in many different forms.

Screeching at each other or refusing to talk when we really should communicate in order to resolve our differences, breathing heavily, holding back or being temperamental in our contact with others, compulsive behaviour, phobias, not letting the other person talk, or poor listening. All these behaviours affect us negatively in the long run.

Our thoughts are negatively affected by prolonged inner stress. It is easy to get bogged down with certain notions and mind traps. Then it is hard to concentrate, and make decisions. We can develop negative feelings about many situations and ourselves. Interaction with our environment will be impaired.

A prolonged, anguish evoking state of alert, let us call it "anxiety-FRAMES", can first arise in specific lifesituations, e.g. at school.

If stress reactions in the body are not reduced by contact and comforting communication with friends, (understanding, relaxation and good sleep) alertness and "anxiety-FRAMES" may be carried into other lifesituations, e.g. down town saturday night. Anxiety may step by step be generalized into other circumstantial conditions.

Negative emotions trigger the brain to search for threatening objects (threatening gestalts, evil eyes, angry voices etc.) in the outer situation, or threatening phenomena (pain, palpitation, heavy breathing etc.) within the body.

The "brain wide web" is searched for all relevant information that may substantiate our fears.

If the brain is then influenced by stress hormones – and maybe afflicted by constricted blood vessels due to hyperventilation – there is a great risk that the search will be biased. Threatening information comes to the fore.

Mind traps are made of psychological FRAMES matter. They are created by stress reflexes and selective perceptions.

When they generate inner stress and when fight-flight responses are not balanced by sufficient relaxation, comforting analysis and communication with other people, constructive daydreaming and good sleep, the body will develop anxiety-related psycho-somatic symptoms.

Inner stress and anguish may then be incorporated into almost every situation in life (generalized anxiety or social phobia).

Chapter 6. Dysfunctional Breathing and Impaired Psychosomatic Function as a result of anguish, stress, pain, fear or anger.

Breathing reactions are thus part of fight-flight reflexes. I can react to paralyzing fear by holding my breath, or I can hyperventilate. Heavy costal breathing can be very disconcerting to say the least – a point readily vouched for by a person who has experienced a panic attack.

Hyperventilation can lead to constricted airways restricting breathing severely (the word anguish comes from the Latin "angustia" meaning narrow passage). The physiological mechanism responsible for this constriction of the airways is mainly due to lack of the gas carbon dioxide.

•We breathe in oxygen and breathe out carbon dioxide (a waste gas) that is continually emitted by the body due to the metabolism of food.

•Carbon dioxide + water = carbonic acid. Compare this to soda water; when the carbon dioxide escapes into the air the acidity disappears.

•The level of carbonic acid affects the blood and the body's pH value. You might be tempted to believe that it would be best to have as much oxygen and as little carbon dioxide as possible left in the body but it is not that simple. As with everything else in nature the human body is subject to mechanisms seeking a natural balance. In unfortunate circumstances the natural balance can be disturbed by an imbalance between oxygen intake and carbon dioxide emission.

The body needs to maintain a certain oxygen level but is also dependant on a certain level of carbon dioxide to keep pH values in balance.

•During normal balanced breathing (adjusted to metabolism) the level of carbon dioxide in the lungs should be approx. 6 %. Carbon dioxide levels in the atmosphere are only 0,037 %. Accordingly carbon dioxide levels in the lungs drop rapidly when we breathe heavily which is what occurs when we have a panic attack. In the alveoli oxygen passes across to the blood and carbon dioxide is passed out from the blood during breathing. When the level of carbon dioxide in the lungs drops, the level of carbonic acid in the blood drops.

•This means that heavy breathing during physical exertion is alright. However heavy breathing without physical exertion and due to agitation is definitely not good. It leads to "respiratory alcholosis" which means that the pH value in the blood becomes basic, something the body does not appreciate. There is now an imbalance in the body's pH value.

•The body defends itself by constricting the smooth muscles in the airways. It becomes hard to breathe leading us to fear; "I can't breathe!" and then we try to breathe even harder. It is a mind trap because we are already breathing too hard. Our forceful, heavy breathing is causing our shortness of breath.

•When I breathe too heavily there is a negative effect on the oxygen supply to all tissue in the body. At lower carbonic acid levels oxygen more readily bonds with haemoglobin in the red blood vessels. Body tissue can therefore not acquire oxygen as easily.

Consequently sufficient carbon dioxide levels provide tissues with easier access to oxygen which in turn affects metabolism on a cellular level positively.

To sum it up: Sufficient levels of carbonic acid lead to better uptake of oxygen in body tissue. The brain is the most important recipient of oxygen and needs a good supply to function effectively.

Experiencing a panic attack is very upsetting. It feels like choking. Your heart is beating hard and fast. You feel dizzy and might also break out in a sweat.

Some people faint. When you faint your "automatic pilot" takes over your body's functions. The heavy breathing is no longer precipitated by the fear "I cannot breathe!". Breathing calms by itself.

People who experience a panic attack for the first time can get so frightened by it that they reorganize their lives in order to avoid experiencing another attack, but their fear for anxiety can in itself bring on a panic attack.

This can lead to social phobia if they do not learn that the attack is a result of stress reflexes and can be relieved by breathing calmly with the diaphragm (stomach breathing).

Most of my patients who have learned about the significance of carbon dioxide have felt relief afterwards. They have an explanation to how the body reacts and why breathing becomes difficult when they feel anxious.

Patients who have undergone a harrowing ambulance trip to the hospital after a panic attack have been referred to the pulmonary clinic for assessment but no problems have been found. They have only been told that they have had a panic attack.

None of those patients I have met with this problem have been informed about how hyperventilation can constrict the airways leading to shortness of breath. Or should I say; if they have received information it has not been remembered. One young man became agitated when he was informed about this at his session with me. He said that he would not have been so worried after examination if he had been informed about it.

A couple of my patients, who have understood the importance of breathing physiology, have been so reassured that they have never experienced a panic attack again.

Others have been in generatized anxiety but have been able to improve by dialectic FRAMES therapy and breathing exercises.

If you live in a prolonged, anguish evoking state of alertness there is a risk that heavy breathing becomes the automatic and normal breathing pattern (hyperventilation syndrome). The respiratory control centre of the brain adjusts to a lower level of carbon dioxide.

"Upside down breathing" is one way to describe chest breathing. You breathe with the help of muscles in the rib cage and shoulders instead of using the diaphragm ("breathing from your stomach"). Your body tries to protect itself from hyperventilation (increase of pH level) by constricting the airways including the nasal passage. When the nose is blocked you breathe through your mouth – which can add to the problem of hyperventilation since it is easier to breathe fast trough an open mouth.

People with chronic hyperventilation often breathe through their mouths. However, the natural path for breathing is through the nose. The nasal passages with their cilia heat up, moisten and cleanse the air as it enters the body. When air is taken in through the mouth it is not cleansed and moistened in the same fashion. If your nose is blocked all year round, even when colds are not prevalent, then you could be a chest breather. There is a good chance that asthma associated with physical exertion is a result of breathing in cold, dry air through the mouth, irritating the mucous membranes which react by emitting histamines. Hyperventilation and contraction of the smooth muscles in the bronchi and alveoli may also contribute to this type of asthma.

Nightmares, worry and anguish can cause us to wake up feeling like we are being suffocated which is a result of chest breathing and hyperventilation during sleep.

Another complication of hyperventilation is fatigue, lack of energy and listlessness. This can be the result of the body's attempt to balance its pH levels by releasing hydrogen ions into the blood stream affecting the body's buffer supply.

Proper breathing technique has interested people throughout history. In Yoga there has, for thousands of years, been a great understanding of the importance of breathing. This knowledge could soon be lost in our modern, stressful society.

However there are signs that people are once again showing interest in the culture and lifestyle of the Far East. Many people in the Western World practise yoga and meditation. The medical world of Western Society places full credence in evidence-based research as basis for treatment of different ailments. Therefore, extensive research is needed about the physiological importance of breathing for our well-being. Lifestyle-related diseases should not only be cured by medicines.

Balanced breathing should primarily match the activity level of the body. Forced breathing due to anger or fear is, in the long run, detrimental to our health. Hyperventilation affects the body's pH balance.

In principle you could say that anger and fear are solely functional for mobilizing energy in preparation for physical exertion. Anger can be advantageous when I have to exert myself physically but it has a negative effect on mental flexibility.

Breathing is regulated by the autonomic nervous system and we are often unaware of our breathing. Therefore, it can be difficult to start thinking about breathing and changing our breathing if it is unbalanced. Masters of Yoga have spent a long time concentrating on their breathing in order to acquire good control of it.

It is important to realize that breathing is a process involving different zones in the body. Chest breathing involves the muscles of the neck, shoulder girdle and rib cage while abdominal breathing involves the diaphragm. The diaphragm is a large dome-shaped muscle lying within the body cavity separating the abdomen from the chest.

The diaphragm is the most important breathing muscle. Its action is automatic. When it contracts it pushes down towards the stomach, causing a drop in pressure within the chest thereby drawing air deep into the lungs.

The diaphragm usually functions automatically but we can control it if we want to and use it to take a voluntary diaphragmatic breath. Thus, breathing can be executed both voluntarily and involuntarily.

Contraction of the diaphragm may often be counteracted by the action of the muscles of the abdominal wall, not least in athletic individuals.

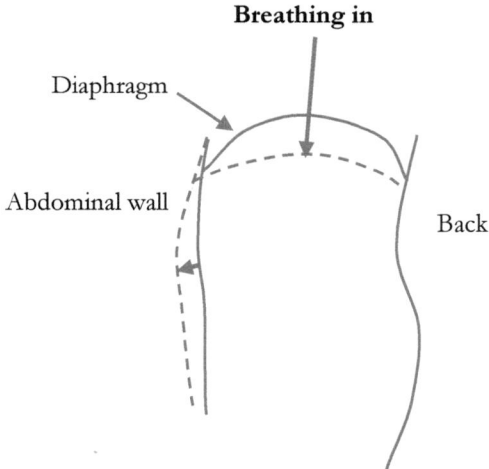

Breathing in

Diaphragm

Abdominal wall

Back

Therefore, the muscles of the abdominal wall (our "muscle corset") should be relaxed when we breathe in, so that the diaphragm muscle can work without resistance. When we breathe out the diaphragm relaxes and at this phase in breathing you may very well contract the "muscle corset" if you wish.

It is almost impossible to breathe in deeply (using the diaphragm) when we lift a heavy weigh, but if we breathe out during the lift – that will actually help us with the lift because we can harness the power of the muscles of the abdominal wall. In my practice I have noticed that quite a few athletic clients suffer from phobias in combination with dysfunctional breathing pattern in stressful situations.

I would like to develop three facets of my own breathing pattern. First, I want my abdomen to be relaxed while I breathe in. One sigh with the diaphragm can really help. Secondly, I strive to breathe through my nose. If I am forced to breathe through my mouth, at least I try to inhale through my nose. Thirdly, I want my breathing to be slow and in accordance with the activity level of my body. If I need to breathe more heavily because I am exerting myself, I increase my breathing only as much as is necessary, not more. We do not increase our ability to act optimally by breathing harder than necessary.

Oxygen intake has to be balanced with carbon dioxide expulsion for the blood's pH level to be optimally balanced as the metabolism works best then. Unbalanced breathing is like a maladjusted carburettor in a car which leads to an unclean engine.

Diaphragm breathing is better than chest breathing because it allows oxygen to reach all the alveoli.

If air is only carried to the central parts of the lungs then there is a smaller interface for diffusion of oxygen into the blood stream. But with slow diaphragm breathing, when you are also using the lower and outer; larger parts of the lungs, you will have a better balance between oxygen intake and carbon dioxide ventilation.

Voluntary, deep slow breathing can help us relax and rest. It can calm the body and even allay palpitations we experience due to stress reflexes and mind traps. If you want to breathe slowly and deeply you should try to reach a feeling of rest and calm inside your stomach at the end of exhalation, before you inhale again.

Experiment with different ways of breathing abdominally to find a slow breathing pattern that suits you. Make it comfortable for yourself!

If you want to develop your ability to breathe calmly, and you are a "chest breather" because of stress at work, stress at home, body building, fear for letting your stomach bulge out, or if you wear clothes that do not allow you to breath with the diaphragm, it can be a long difficult process to become a "diaphragm breather". I know, because I have been a chest breather myself.

If you breathe a lot with your chest and start exercising diaphragm breathing, you may feel like driving a car with a reversed mechanism in the steering wheel – when you steer to the right the car drives to the left. Quite a few patients tense their abdominal wall, expand their chest and lift their shoulders when I ask them to take a deep breath. Pain in the chest, neck and shoulders can originate from rib cage and shoulder girdle movements and tense diaphragm muscle.

Here are some breathing exercises that can be useful. Put one hand on your stomach and one hand on your chest and pay attention to which hand is moving as you breathe – during good diaphragm breathing the hand on the stomach moves.

It is important that your clothes do not restrain your breathing when you do these exercises: Sit or lie down and "breathe with your stomach" (not with your chest).

Continue for a couple of minutes and explore the relaxation in your body. You can choose to breathe six breaths per minute (ten seconds per breath) to increase your awareness of your breathing speed. Can you do this easily?

Six breaths per minute is slow breathing, because we usually breathe nine to twentyfour breaths per minute, depending on how hard we work with our muscles. But six breaths per minute is quite natural if we are at rest, sitting or lying down. If you do not manage six breaths per minute perhaps you can manage eight breaths per minute (about tree seconds in and four seconds out).

When time for breathing out (plus relaxation at the end of exhalation) is longer than time for inhalation, it is a sign of relaxation in the diaphragm at the end of exhalation. Some patients cannot reach that relaxed feeling in the stomach at the end of exhalation, probably because of a tense diaphragm. Those patients can suffer from pain in their chests and/or pain in their backs where the diaphragm attaches to the rib cage.

If you want to try to breathe about six breaths per minute – remember to breathe with your stomach! (Holding one hand right over the diaphragm and one hand on your chest will help).

The goal is to decrease your breathing frequency, and to increase the volume of your breaths by using more of the lower, more voluminous parts of your lungs.

This can only be done during diaphragm breathing. Any degree of breathing speed reduction is a success if you are a "hyper ventilator". I recommend that you make it a routine to breathe calmly with your stomach for a while, every morning and every night.

Whenever you experience a stress reflex, take notice of whether your breathing goes up into the chest. If so, concentrate on getting it back into the stomach.

If you stand in a queue waiting for your turn and feel irritated, and your breathing turns into chest breathing, try this exercise: Let your stomach swell when you inhale – then exhale while you compress your abdominal wall like when you blow out all the lights on a birthday cake. This way you can reach two goals; exercising your abdominal wall and reducing breathing speed – while at the same time exercising rhythmic collaboration of the diaphragm and the abdominal wall.

To sum it up: Breathe with the diaphragm and breathe slowly. If you allow your abdomen to really swell during inhalation you can fill the lower bulkier part of your lungs more effectively. Thereby you can breathe calmer and it will be easier to rest your breathing muscles at the end of exhalation. That will lower your heart rate and your body can relax.

Chapter 7. Depression or Passion for life

Stress reflexes and mind traps can gradually take so much energy that the body becomes exhausted and you can fall into depression and thus limit creativity and openness for life. Inner stress levels can get very high from time to time. This is why depressed individuals may experience a hyper sensitivity for sensory stimuli. Eventually you cannot handle increased stress. The slightest exertion can be equated with climbing a mountain or running a marathon.

The executive, planning, thinking and processing parts of the brain can no longer perform their functions, while the deeper central parts of the brain, those responsible for energy regulation, are unable to coordinate energy regulation appropriate to the situation at hand. The depressed individual finds it difficult to focus mentally and can therefore easily get laden down with worrying thoughts about himself or about how life should be.

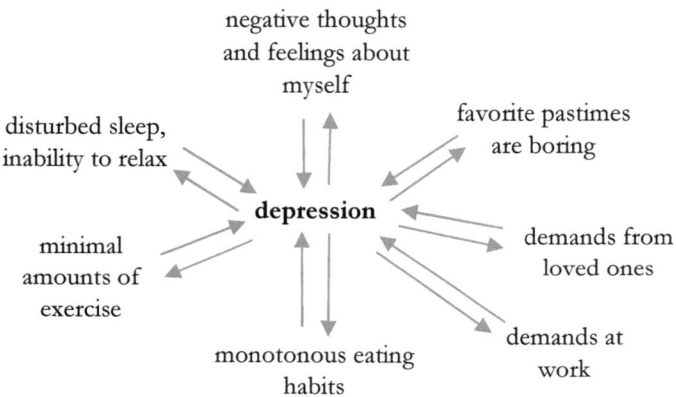

If you think positively about yourself you can fight depression. However, if you are depressed you find it almost impossible to think positively about yourself or your life. Your body uses sleep and relaxation to recuperate (the body repairs any damage, builds up energy depots and enhances the immune system) thereby deterring depression. The problem is that when you are depressed you usually cannot relax and may find it hard to sleep and convalesce.

Physical exercise leaves us warm and relaxed and we usually feel good after exertion. The problem is that when we are depressed we usually cannot find the motivation to exercise. To eat regularly and have a balanced diet is a deterrent to depression.

However, when you are depressed you find it difficult to eat regularly and sensibly because you do not experience a normal appetite. You are inclined to take the easiest option, such as fast-food, which contains a lot of fast acting carbohydrates that supply the brain with energy quickly but which are quickly expended leaving you tired and drowsy afterwards.

An inspiring job and getting on well at work can protect you from depression. On the other hand, if you are depressed any job can be like torture. When you get on well with friends and your loved ones you find it easier to avoid depression but if you are depressed you are more inclined to get into arguments and conflicts with friends and family. A special interest or hobby will increase your passion for life but if you are already depressed not even a favourite hobby seems like fun.

Troubling thoughts hamper sleep and if they reappear in dreams they may thwart the body's deep sleep recovery. This leads to memory and concentration problems during the day. That in turn causes more stress as daily activities do not go well.

Recent scientific research shows that daily exercise is just as effective as the latest antidepressant medicines against mild to moderate depression. Physical activity during the day helps us relax and makes it easier to fall asleep when bedtime comes. Our bodies are essentially designed to be physically active. Hormone expenditure is tailored to a life of physical activity coupled with sufficient sleep and relaxation.

Sleep hormone cycles vary in a constant pattern over a twentyfour hour day. For eons evolution has continued without electricity to light up the night. Metabolism of sleep hormones is adjusted to that. Sleep should occur during the same period every day so that melatonin works properly. The melatonin cycle functions best if the body is subjected to sunlight during the day.

If you spend enough time lying in bed awake worrying and fretting about your inability to sleep you will eventually associate bed with a state of worry. Therefore, it is important not to exacerbate the negative association with bed by using it as a "boring TV-couch" or a place where you do office work. Bed must be a symbol for pleasure and relaxation. If you cannot sleep, get up and do something else. Bed should be reserved for sleep (or sex).

A balanced metabolism requires a balanced diet. A balanced diet, including vitamins and minerals, ensures that bodily functions remain stable and steady. The problem with the fight-flight reflex is that it leads to temporary cessation of the digestive process. Loss of appetite and onesided food intake are risks during prolonged periods of stress.

Numerous vicious circles are present in a state of depression which is a prime example of the relationship between body and soul.

Physical exhaustion due to prolonged stress without recuperation affects behaviour, sensual focus, the thought process, feelings and how we see ourselves.

Mental Stability is dependant on

Physical Stability

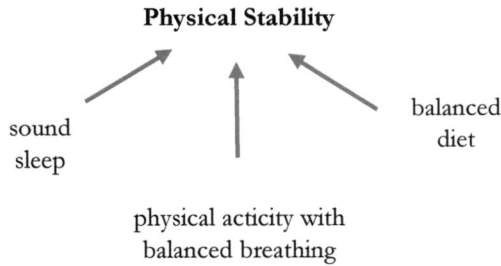

sound
sleep

balanced
diet

physical acticity with
balanced breathing

Since the human psyche is a *cyclical system* one can also say that the **reverse** correlation is true.

Physical Stability is dependant on

Mental Stability

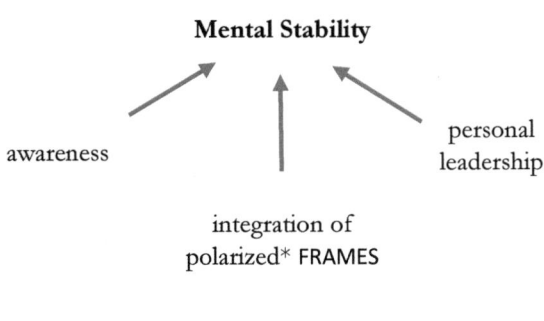

awareness

personal
leadership

integration of
polarized* FRAMES

* see Chapter 9 (Polarized **FRAMES**)

To be in charge of your sleeping, eating, exercising and breathing habits you need to be able to control your focus of attention, your mental focus and your focus of action (see Appendix about balanced FRAMES). In summary: Depression, besides leading to social and mental problems, leads to difficulties with food intake, sleep and exercise. Instead we can reverse this train of thought and stipulate how we would like things to be, how vicious circles are reversed to good circles:

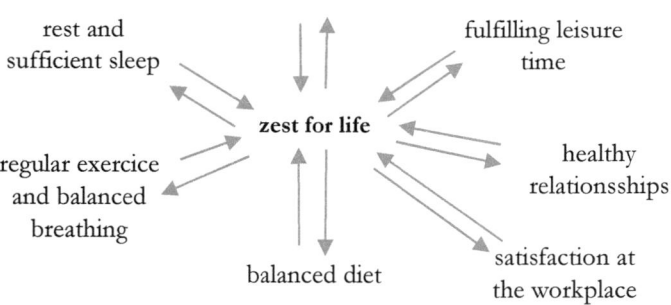

All of these elements, social, mental, emotional and physical are important for our passion for life. Improving any one of these elements will enhance our lives. It is important to see the whole picture and acknowledge the importance of each one of these intrinsic elements in creating a zest for life.

Any improvement of any one of these factors is valuable even if it does not, in itself, lead to the goal of complete happiness.

In time, improvements in any of these facets of life can lead to positive results that can replace vicious circles with good, positive circles, thereby improving satisfaction with life as a whole.

In life there is a constant transition between exertion and rest, stress and recuperation. Muscles contract and relax; the heart and breathing are symbols for this. Sensory impressions and the brains interpretation of them need variation to be clear in our consciousness.

The body's different needs are also a pulsation between satisfaction and dissatisfaction. Hunger – contention, energy – fatigue, movement – rest. Feelings come and go.

The FRAMES system pulsates with life and reactions in the body. Focus of attention, reactions in the body, action, mental focusing, emotions and our view of ourselves are represented from one point to another like clouds in the sky or waves in the water. They keep coming and going.

Passion for life necessitates that our life is good enough to allow gratification and happy thoughts about the future prevail. When negative thoughts and stressors prevail mental focus and sensory focus will be on that which troubles us, and personal development is at risk of being stunted. Personal leadership, taking responsibility for your own life, the ability to make contact with others, integrity and creativity can all be at risk when psychosomatic burdens reign for a long time.

Chapter 8. Unique FRAMES of the Individual

Imagine that the components of FRAMES are bobbins in a weaving machine and the machinery constantly creates a long "tapestry of life".

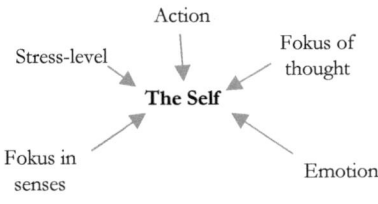

Every individual weaving machine is creating a unique fabric because the social situation is unique to every individual.

In light of the fact that each human being is unique, with unique experiences, every one of us has created a unique tapestry that is relevant to our particular constellation of FRAMES.

Bodily reactions, that are fundamental for how we feel, are affected by what thoughts and impressions we focus on.

Experiences become a blend of thoughts and impressions from our outer surrounding zone and expressions from inside our bodies. The image in the mirror shows the picture I have of myself but also "the social mirrors" give me a picture of how other people see me. Thoughts about my future and my past, of how I behave, give me a picture of "who I am" in my social network.

Life consists of an enormous amount of psychological FRAMES. – Like the frames in a film, many FRAMES are almost inseparable from each other. Therefore, it is not surprising that they become, more or less, automatic.

Daily experiences usually follow the same patterns week in and week out. When we learn to ride a bicycle we are well aware of how we hold our hands on the handle bars and feet on the peddles, how we keep our balance and the pride we feel when we can ride our bicycle. After a while, when we get better at riding the bicycle, we divert our attention from the physical act of riding and start focusing on traffic instead.

In the same way as cycling develops from conscious physical action to automatic subconscious action, the act of living life develops. A lot of things become subconscious and we turn our attention to new things.

Fundamental experiences of how to relate to others, how we feel, how we act and think begin early in life. Trust, mistrust or conflicting feelings are present from an early age and can become automatic, turning them into subconscious reflexes and mind patterns.

If I am unaware of my automatic reactions there is a greater risk that they will dictate how I form my life without my realizing it.

When I started working as a psychologist in the seventies, meeting a psychologist was considered taboo and was something most people were ashamed of. This has changed in recent years and I am happy about that, but it is still not unusual that people are ashamed.

I think it is not strange at all, that people feel apprehensive about going to a psychologist to talk about their problems. This is actually quite logical. It is not hard to understand that you can react with stress, because just thinking about your problems, past and present, or those you fear in the future, leads to worry and stress. It is natural that you wish to avoid talking about your mental pain and the problems you have, as this is hard work and may involve anxiety.

However it can also be cathartic to talk about your problems. If the therapist understands, if the session goes better than you expected or if you acquire new liberating thoughts, insights and feelings that you did not have before, you may feel more hopeful about the future.

Once I saw the following text in a comic strip: "I have absolutely no confidence in a person who chooses to hang out with someone like myself." This is a witty line that houses a deeper, serious sentiment. If you have felt out of place and that has characterized your inner impression of yourself as being not wanted, this mind trap is not illogical at all. Feeling ostracized you wonder why people turn their backs on you.

When you think about how other people do not like you, you get a pain in your stomach or other fight-flight reactions. When the body experiences stress symptoms, there is a greater risk that you assume that other people distain you. You then make the wrong conclusions and wind up in a mind trap: Why should they like me when I do not even like myself?

Episodes that are embarrassing, uncomfortable or stressful as well as occurrences that feel good can all be analyzed using the FRAMES list, whether they occurred recently or many years ago.

F What did you see or hear? What in particular did you notice? What did you focus on?

R How did your body react?

A How did you act in this situation?

M What was your mental reaction? What did you think?

E What did you feel? What emotional condition did you end up in?

S What impression did you have of yourself? What happened to your self-esteem and self-confidence?

When a client in therapy tells about an episode, the therapist may ask: What are your feelings right now when you tell me this? This question will help the client to relate to the FRAMES of that particular episode, by transfer into the present, here and now, in a more secure context.

During therapy we become conscious of ourselves and all the automated reflexes that still control our lives, thereby making it easier to choose, in a more enlightened way, what to think and how to act.

The self is made up of your past life, your belief of what the future holds and what you want to do with your life right now. The story of your life "changes" when it is told.

Earlier parts of our tapestries may be "unfinished business" or "mind traps". Gestalts in the story may be fragmented and must be completed before we can "digest" them and integrate them into our creative learning personality. The circumstances of earlier traumatic events may have to be "filled in" so we can see the whole picture.

Remember the formula: O – [FRAMES] – EO, where O stands for "Outer situation" including other people's FRAMES, and EO stands for effects of FRAMES on the outer, external situation.

Analysis matrix:

The systemic interaction between F, R, A, M, E and S can be described and analyzed as follows:

A-level: Dynamics between the different components of FRAMES? How does stress level affect strenght of anxiety? How does stress level affect mental reasoning? Etc.

B-level: How integrated or dissociated are different FRAMES within one and the same individual? For instance how "the child within" make an adult dysfunctional in social settings? (Inner conflicts and dilemmas).

C-level: Social interaction on a group level (a dyad, a triad etc.). How does the behaviour of one individual affect the action of another individual?

D-level: How for instance selective perception and action of an individual is a function of social trends (analysis on a sociological level).

If an individual experience psychological trauma in life he/she may dissociate, insted of associating and integrating within the self, memories associated to the trauma.

Dissociation at the A-level: for instance *not acting* upon *thought* or *emotion* or *not acting* in acordance with the *actual situation.*

66

Or dissociation at the *B-level*. Whole parts of the self are not associated – different parts of the self "argue" (for instance "the grown up self" is overwhelmed by "the child within" so that he/she cannot take adult responcibility in the situation).

At the *C-level* (contact human to human being) suffer from distrust and bad communication.

It has been some years since I worked in family therapy settings. At that time I had not developed the psycho educative framework of the FRAMES model, but I am confident that a psycho educative approach will work in a family therapy process as I have experienced that at the youth centre where the model was developed in gestalt therapy with teenagers.

It is not common practice that parents come to our youth centre, but it happens and clients have expressed appreciation of the fact that their parents have a better understanding of their symptoms after being informed of the mechanisms of depression or anxiety within the frame-work of the FRAMES model.

When we see early parts of our tapestries more clearly it will have an impact on how we weave our future tapestry. Earlier shortcomings will not torture us in the same way any more. We have a better understanding and feel calmer.

During therapy, when headway is being made, clients commonly ask when they continue to suffer from stressreflexes: "How should I think about this?" They realize that they still experience stress reflexes despite having changed their behaviour and the way they think. They expect to solve their problems by thinking properly and acting in an appropriate manner.

If remaining stressreflexes are at the A-level my answer to them is: "It is merely a reflex". You have to accept that it takes time for the stress reflexes to disappear even though you might think that everything is much better now. You can compare this to Pavlov's dogs (see chapter 10 Learned Stress reflexes and mind traps). Reflexes that are automated remain until they are replaced by other reflexes.

If problems are at B or C-level analyzing FRAMES may be more complex.

Chapter 9. Polarized FRAMES

When a little child is satisfied it can love its mother. However, if it is dissatisfied it experiences its mother in a completely different way. Part of a child's development involves it eventually coming to terms with the fact that its mother sometimes says "yes" and other times says "no" and in time learning to accept that. The child's relationship with its mother is not jeopardized despite temporarily being denied this or that.

The child needs to appreciate that everything will be alright despite being denied what it wants from its mother. The child has developed a sense of "love trust" when it can grasp that the object for love (mother or father) will stay and take care of it even though it is being denied something at the present moment.

Soon the child understands even more about its attachment to – and its cooperation with its mother, which is the "prototype" for relationships with other human beings. In order to trust what another person says, you need to be able to believe that he or she really means it when he/she says "yes" or "no".

All the sensory input the child receives about how the other person is feeling and thinking should correlate with what they are actually saying, for the child to learn how to interact with others.

69

If the child receives conflicting signals from the other person it will feel torn and uncertain of how to act.

I conducted a FRAMES analysis on one of my patients, a young man worried about his mother, with whom he no longer lived. This happened about ten years ago when he was nine years old:

His *focus*; mother tells him: "Mammy loves you! You know that you can always come to me if something is troubling you".

Reactions within the body; "I then feel calm and relaxed".

Actions; "I help mother all the time. I want her to be happy with me".

Mental conceptions; "I think she loves me".

Emotions and the impression we have of ourselves; "I love her".

Then his mother, who is an alcoholic, had a relapse and started to drink again.

Focus; "she starts to drink again". "I'll be there at your graduation", she says but she never turns up.

Reactions within the body; "I feel a pain in my stomach, my head aches and I cannot sleep".

Actions; flight behaviour; dishonest responses to the question "how are you?"

Mental conceptions; "I believe she doesn't want me anymore".

Emotions and the impression we have of ourselves; "I am ashamed. I felt violated".

Polarized FRAMES:

(F) Focus in senses: My mother loves me.

(F) Focus in senses: She starts to drink again

(R) Relaxation

(R) Fight Flight

(A) I help her. I want her to be happy.

(A) Dishonest respons to "how are you?"

(M) I think she loves me

(M) She does´t love me.

(E) I love her.

(E) I´m ashamed

(S) Trust

(S) Distrust

His perception of his mother was split into two completely different FRAMES.

He felt security and trust when he heard his mother say "Mammy loves you! You know that you can always come to me if something is troubling you". He felt calm and was certain that his mother really loved him.

However, when his mother started drinking again he could only feel deceived and lack of trust for his mother. He felt a nagging sense of anxiety all day long. He was not truthful when his mother asked him how he felt – the few times she actually asked. He tried to flee from the whole situation, both mentally and physically, believing that she did not want him anymore.

The impression he had about himself: "Nobody wants me, not even my own mother!" This made it impossible for him to feel selfconfident which is tantamount for the development of a healthy self-esteem. It became impossible for him to integrate these two conflicting impressions of his mother to a whole experience of his mother that was satisfactory. He became distrustful of the whole world and himself.

The impression we have of ourselves can be like a mosaic of conflicting FRAMES that contradict each other; for example we can seem to be in control but at the same time be lost, seem confident then suddenly afraid. This is a very difficult situation to handle.

When we feel like a stressed, violated child on the inside we experience a fight-flight situation which is exacerbated by an invasive perception of parental indifference making the whole experience almost unbearable.

If someone says "Why are you sitting here sulking?" you feel guilty and ashamed. If someone tries to comfort you, you do not know whether to trust them or not. You feel confused. You cannot appreciate the words of comfort from someone who is genuinely concerned about you and thereby you may lose that persons support. You find it hard to differentiate between genuine concern and accusation.

Development of personal integrity may be negatively affected by such ambiguous FRAMES, but on the other hand, life experiences like these can also, later in life, in a supportive environment be processed into wisdom and personal integrity.

Integration of polarities (polarized FRAMES) is an aspect of personal development.

Personality trait continuums like generous–stingy, aggressive–timid, extrovert–introvert, ambitious–let go attitude, trustful–distrustful etc. may all be affected by experiences in our formative years.

But as we become wiser, in new circumstances, we can broaden our FRAMES repertoire into "in between behaviours" where we can see things from different angles, trusting our own integrity.

Chapter 10. Learned Stress Reflexes and Mind Traps

What does the words "learned stress reflex" mean? The expression is based on the notion of a "conditioned" reflex (to be precise conditional response or situation reflex). A reflex that has originated from specific circumstances. The expression was coined during Ivan Pavlov's research of the digestive reflexes of dogs at the end of the 18th century. Salivation is an inherent reflex that takes place when dogs eat food.

However, salivation that occurs when a dog only sees the laboratory assistant who usually comes with food for him is a programmed, conditioned reflex. Pavlov experimented with different visual and aural impressions (circles, bells, tuning forks etc.) that he presented at the same time as the dogs were fed.

The dogs then learned to associate sounds or visual impressions with food. This resulted in their salivating merely because they saw a circle or heard a certain sound even though they did not actually see or taste food. Pavlov elicited in this way a *conditioned reflex* in the dogs.

Pavlov's research was primarily concerned with digestion but conditioning of reflexes can even be evoked for flight or fight or desire and enjoyment. If your boss has told you off, the sound of his steps can trigger a stress reflex for example.

Is it possible to decrease or completely extinguish a conditioned reflex? For example "pain in the stomach" when you have to stand on stage and hold a lecture.

Yes it is possible. You have to focus on new conditioning of reflexes and behaviour that is associated with standing on stage and giving a lecture. If you practice and subject yourself to holding lectures at the same time as you shift your focus of attention and focus of mind; new FRAMES can develop. If you praise yourself, or somebody else does, because of something you have done, you can gradually see the whole situation in a new light.

Your body feels different; the lecture hall feels different which is a result of your undergoing an "operant" virginal understanding.

The old troublesome stress reflex (pain in the stomach) can possibly resurface when you are depressed or dispirited. On the other hand, it might disappear completely. When you have understood and "forgiven" the dynamics of your nervous FRAMES´ vicious circles – and you are aware of the dynamics of your new, more relaxed FRAMES – your awareness can act as an "antidote" against possible relapse. It is important to continue to praise yourself for the progress you have made.

Many problems originate during childhood. Of course, you can say that the only thing that is important is the present, and that is, indeed, true in a way.

However, if what happened in your childhood still affects you today, as conditioned stress reflexes, it is important to be aware of that and to realize your ability to choose your reaction in certain situations.

It can be cathartic to discuss earlier experiences in life and your fundamental FRAMES. For my part, I finally made the connection when I had ruminated about a PowerPoint presentation that I had to make about the FRAMES process, with particular attention to "reaction within the body". I got all worked up about something my wife said.

Afterwards, having calmed down, and looked back on my reaction, I understood how my stress reflexes had dictated my thoughts and actions during my formative years.

With this insight I gained perspective into early experiences in life that had made their mark and had now, without warning, reappeared as stress reflexes.

I could now analyze the situation; "that was then, now I am in a totally different phase of life – I have a better understanding of the situation and I am not so vulnerable and helpless as before." As a result of this emotional breakthrough I dreamt about puzzle bits falling into place in front of my eyes. The insight I gained lead to normalization of my high blood pressure.

To capitalize on such breakthroughs you need to practice the new way of thinking and acting over and over again. A mental association, negative or positive, that is relived every day, week and month over a period of years, finally becomes like a motorway in the brain. New thoughts that have not been versed as many times as the old ones are barely recognizable trodden pathways in comparison. These new pathways need to be trodden upon countless times to feel as reliable as the motorways.

One prerequisite for developing a more genuine contact with yourself and others is to respect how your body reacts – to be aware of stress reflexes and relaxation responses. You have to understand what makes you feel bad and how to deal with it in order to feel relaxed and gain better self-esteem. Feeling good or bad depends on how you think about things, the way you act and how you see the world.

Our mental capacity, our ability to envisage different courses of events can be both an asset and a liability. In therapy thoughts can be "examined" on face value and for how they are thought: What am I thinking? And how am I thinking these thoughts? Automated and subconscious? With focus on details? Generalizations? Creative new thinking? Are my thoughts negative or positive? Are my thoughts ensnared in mind traps?

Mind traps keep stress reflexes alive as long as they are not uncovered as the treacherous mind traps they, in fact, are. Finding yourself in a mind trap is finding yourself caught in an inescapable vicious circle of stressful thoughts that go round and round.

Mind traps act as traps because they lead to stress reflexes that limit mental focus. Inner stress is the basis for phobias, anxiety, paranoia, compulsive behaviour, compulsive thinking, depression and other anxiety related conditions.

The following figure (next page) is an example of how stress reflexes and mind traps affect each other. It shows how a thought can arouse and perpetuate stress reflexes as well as how stress reflexes can awaken and keep mind traps alive.

Vicious mental circles often originate from some worrying thought for example "What if I have cancer!".

stress reflexes	mind trap

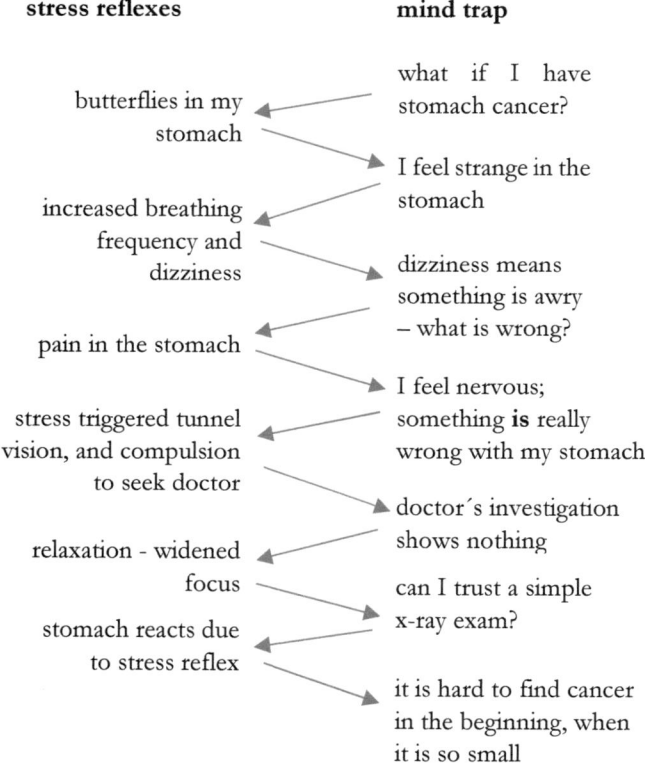

stress reflexes

butterflies in my stomach

increased breathing frequency and dizziness

pain in the stomach

stress triggered tunnel vision, and compulsion to seek doctor

relaxation - widened focus

stomach reacts due to stress reflex

mind trap

what if I have stomach cancer?

I feel strange in the stomach

dizziness means something is awry – what is wrong?

I feel nervous; something **is** really wrong with my stomach

doctor´s investigation shows nothing

can I trust a simple x-ray exam?

it is hard to find cancer in the beginning, when it is so small

In this way a phobia, that you have a disease, can manifest itself. The vast majority of my patients who suffer from different phobias and compulsive thoughts are not aware that their troubles, by and large, are caused by the body's stress reflexes.

If you can decrease corporal stress in these situations then you will diminish the severity of the mind trap.

The following is an example of a mind trap that hinders sleep and leads to insomnia:

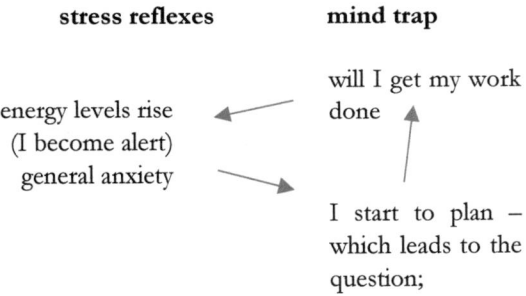

stress reflexes

energy levels rise
(I become alert)
general anxiety

mind trap

will I get my work done

I start to plan – which leads to the question;

The typical thing about mind traps is that they often arise from inner stress and that the thoughts that are generated add even more to inner stress levels. They act as shackling negative spirals of limiting thought associations and stress reactions. Exhaustion makes it even more difficult to get priorities right.

Mind traps can concern anything, but the power of the trap is due to the stress reflex that limits our vision to what we are scared of or angry at.

The automatic filtered, selective or uncertain focus makes it difficult for us to escape from the mind trap.

The diagram below illustrates a FRAMES analysis of claustrophobia (an athletic man who feels dizzy as the walls "fall down on him" when he uses the elevator).

Claustrophobia:

F: neither adequate inner focus; to cope with body sensations – nor steady external focus to process outer sensory input

R: flight reflex

A: flight action

M: I will have a panic attack in the elevator! I will not be able to breathe!

E: irritation, fear

Here are some examples of automated distortions in thinking inspired by Judith Beck's book "Cognitive therapy, Basics and beyond". The distortions are due to thoughts and sensory impressions being experienced with limited filters (coloured glasses).

All-or-nothing thinking: It's enough for me to pour a half teaspoon of sugar into my cup to come to the decision that I might as well eat the whole box of chocolates even though I hadn't originally intended to. It's as though I forget that I have partially succeeded and could do even better as time goes on (young woman with eating disorder).

Catastrophizing: What if ….? Most thoughts of catastrophe start with the words "what if" … What if they become furious when I tell them this?

Discounting the positive: It was pure luck that I got on well in the exam.

Emotional reasoning: I feel like I will not succeed. There's no point in my even trying.

Labeling: I'm weird, I'm ugly, I'm boring, I'm a failure etc.

Minimization: That's nothing; others have done much, much cooler things.

Selective abstraction: One of my fifteen work colleagues doesn't like me – "I'm a failure at work".

Mind reading: Mother said that I ate well today. (But I misinterpret her as meaning that I have eaten too much. She really meant that I have eaten healthily.)

Overgeneralization: You can't trust men.

Personalization: Unreasonable habit of believing that it's my fault when someone is irritated and out of balance.

"Should" and "must" statements: I have to fix this because no one else will.

Tunnel vision: The *only* thing that helps is ...

Mind traps readily give rise to behavioural boomerangs. When mind traps dictate my behaviour people around me act accordingly. If I project a low profile in the company of a group of people – because I don't believe they will listen to me anyway – they will not be inclined to listen to me

The result of my behaviour will come back to me like a boomerang. Mental distortions are kept alive by the mechanisms of stress. Selective focus on impressions leads us to concentrate on things that confirm what we believe.

The fight-flight reaction can be transferred, from the subject that originally generated the fear or aggression, to something quite different; a person, a thing, an occurrence etc. They will then unjustly be singled out as targets for my irritation. I may focus on negative characteristics of my target leading to unjust irritation.

Chapter 11. Consequences at group level

Stress reflexes and mind traps have consequences at group level. Fight-flight reflexes caused by ostracism can develop within groups of three or more persons. It is irrelevant if the group is real or imaginary. Stress reflexes due to rivalry can be activated in imaginative scenarios as well. Jealousy can be described in the following manner:

F - You focus on indications that your friend likes someone else, overlooking that your friend actually likes you better.

R - You get a pain in your stomach and feel irritated

A - You become aggressive and behave as if you owned your friend or you avoid the situation by fleeing.

M - You fantasize about how your friend cuddles someone else.

E - You feel worried and irritated.

S - Your self-esteem suffers as a result of your feeling cheated on.

Triangle dramas can present themselves in many different family or group constellations: A child feeling excluded because of it's parents' togetherness, the father feeling excluded by the mother's bond with her child, a sibling feeling excluded because of the father's camaraderie with a brother, a sibling feeling out of place because of the rapport between it's other siblings etc.

Any group constellation with more than two individuals may lead to triangulation – within a family, at school and at work etc. In order to develop into a secure and confident person you need to understand how stress reflexes affect your focus, the way you think, act and feel. This understanding can then develop into trustful relations, with a feeling of self-worth, comfort and relaxation.

Stress reflexes and mind traps can lead to suspicion and hate between groups or fractions within groups. Due to our own group fears and focus on negative impressions about other groups, distorted notions about their thoughts, intentions and actions flourish. Furthermore, the fear of being wrong on an issue (or having an opinion contrary to that of my own group) may cause mental rigidity and mind traps leading to fight or flight behaviour in discussions and debates.

One of the implications of this is that mass media has a great responsibility to openly, objectively and fairly describe the complexities of modern society. Fear of falling numbers of viewers and newspaper readers can lead to tunnel vision – filtering of news and biased reporting by mass media when audience and circulation numbers are the motivating force.

Conflicts of interest between individuals in a group, or between different groups, can be financial or due to desire for power or status. These conflicts have a propensity to distort the way those involved think. They tend to hear and see selectively.

If the leaders of society cultivate feelings of fear between individuals or between groups, there is a risk for stress reflexes and mind traps.

F - You focus on the other group's aggression.

R - Your body experiences a fight-flight response; irritation or fear.

A - You debate aggressively or avoid confrontation.

M - You fantasize about how the other group is going to gain advantage at your group's expense.

E - You feel fear and hate.

S - Self-assertion within the group grows. "We-versus-them-feelings" are fuelled.

If the group leader is a despot he will generate an uneasy group where bullying is prevalent. Those who feel insecure focus on the group leader. A despot generates insecurity whereas a good leader creates a secure atmosphere.

As a school psychologist I have noticed that a lot of children are obsessed with the thought of having a good relationship with the leader (even if he or she is a despot). Although they have the opportunity to be with good friends, they will be more inclined to join "the despot" within the group.

It takes a lot to lead a group of 20 to 30 people which is the size of an average school class. There are not many 7-15 year-olds who have developed such leadership traits. To succeed they have to be able to put aside their own stress reflexes and mind traps and concentrate on good leadership.

If the atmosphere in a class is insecure it is a sign that neither the formal leaders (teachers) nor the informal leaders among the pupils have enough leadership skills to create a safe feeling.

A lot of literature has been written on how the relationship between a child and its parents affects the development of the child's personality. The relationship between children in school classes has not been analyzed in such detail. Swedish school children often go to school together for nine to ten years. These years are important for the development of the student's personality.

In my dealings with youths and adults I have learned that when people feel left out, or feel that they are not allowed to be a part of a group, their personal development is profoundly affected. Stress reflexes and mind traps can for example be characterized as follows:

F - Focus on body language, alliances and how the others see me.

R - I am tense – I have a pain in my stomach.

A - I keep a low profile. I speak when spoken to but do not initiate conversation.

M - I believe that everyone thinks I am boring.

E - I feel worried.

S - My self-esteem is at its lowest.

Stress reflexes diminish creativity and ability to concentrate on school subjects. If a student feels insecure his focus will be on what is worrying him. Therefore, it is of uttermost importance that students feel secure and relaxed at school in order to reach the goals the school has set for them.

Chapter 12. How to handle Mind Traps and Learned Stress Reflexes

The following are some examples of how to deal with everyday stress reflexes, thereby obviating the risk of being ensnared by mind traps. The list follows the FRAMES model:

Focus of attention: The amount of sensory stimuli that in theory might reach our senses widely exceeds the amount of sensory impressions that in reality come to our attention. The selective process continues to select what will be reflected upon in conscious awareness. The brain has a selective capacity that is essential for mental health.

Placid quiet surroundings can be a relief because when we are stressed this capacity to select sensory stimuli may be distorted. Then we may be distracted in our capacity to focus – either we focus too narrowly or we cannot focus at all.

When you feel stressed, try to change your focus, either to something within yourself (e.g. calm breathing) or something outside yourself. When I do the shopping after work I have only one focus i.e. to get it done quickly so I can go home as fast as possible and relax. This focus is particularly evident when I am at the check-out. I try to determine which of the six queues is moving fastest.

I may change queues because another one is faster and then discover that the queue I left is now moving faster. I get frustrated and start to develop tunnel vision. My sole focus is the speed of the queue and this stresses me.

However, I can change focus if I want to and extricate myself from this filtered focus. Instead, I can concentrate on how I am standing; am I comfortable? If not I try to stand comfortably. This will allow me to relax. I can now read the headlines of the papers in the paper rack or think about nice things that make me feel better – I can begin to relax even though I'm in the queue.

Bodily reactions: Inner stress (fight-flight-response) leads to mobilization for physical exertion.

It is beneficial and healthy to channel this mobilization into performing physical exercise in order to metabolize your inner stress. Blood sugars are combusted and adrenaline is expended.

It is then easier for the muscles to relax, the heart to beat more calmly and breathing to become balanced. Leaving the situation in order to take a walk can work miracles. Taking enough breaks at work and obtaining sufficient sleep at night are two important factors to keep stress levels down.

If you suffer from phobia – experiment with your stress reflexes when you get aroused. You might need the support of a therapist but you can do a lot by yourself.

You can treat a spider phobia by looking at a spider; allowing yourself to get afraid – then calm down and take control over your breathing and breathe slowly with your diaphragm, then get afraid again – calm down and so on.

In this way you can gradually take control over your stress reflexes and reduce your helplessness. Rehearse, in full acceptance, that it is not the spider per se that is the problem – it is your disability to handle your stress reflex – the flight response controls your action – and recognize that you have been unable to focus accurately enough to decide whether you are looking at a harmless spider or at a tarantula (a poisonous spider).

Many phobias work this way. The issue is not in the outer zone – the problem is that stress reflexes operate in the inner zone. If your focus of attention is in the outer zone – while the real drama is going on in your body – your attention is led astray.

Action: Experiment with new ways of behaving. Help each other to reflect your behaviour in a generous, respectful and supportive way. As we are often governed by old habits we will, time and again, experience the same results of our behaviour. Chances are small that we will change our behaviour and experience new effects of our behaviour.

Therefore, it is hard to imagine living in a totally different way. To examine new possibilities, afforded by different behaviour and its consequences, you can for example arrange a "polarity party" for friends. Everybody is encouraged to act in a totally different way from how they normally would carry on, to act in a way that is completely opposite to their everyday behaviour.

They should behave that way during the whole party. You will find it very interesting. Since automated thoughts are related to our behaviour we must question these thoughts in order to change our behaviour and act differently.

Mental focus and mind traps: Analyze and process thoughts by examining your thought patterns and mind traps. If you repeat (rehearse) a dysfunctional thought often enough (e.g. it's no use trying to…), say three to ten times a day, you will eventually end up firmly believing that there is no use trying.

If you repeat; "there is no threat to the environment" enough times you might start feeling comfortable with that statement.

When you are unhappy or stressed you experience tunnel vision and filter what you hear, thereby easily finding yourself caught in limiting, ensnaring automated mind traps. "Typically me – as soon as I have to speak in front of a large group I get all worked up and get stuck in a rut".

In order to work through these mind traps you have to look for different logical flaws in these mind traps that block your creativity. Mind traps are usually self-learned and often develop when you are lonely and worried.

However, you can also "inherit" them from your relatives and friends.

How can you question the truth in your automated mind traps? The first step is to realize and admit "that I have, most likely, been caught in a mind trap". Not until you have become aware of a mind trap and have admitted that it is a trap can you start to deal with it.

You can begin by writing down your negative thoughts to see what thought patterns you have. Then you can start to examine the evidence that supports these negative thoughts.

Instead of assuming that your thoughts are true you can examine how plausible they are. Maybe you have a *feeling* that they are reasonable and therefore you *think* they are reasonable.

You can ask yourself: "Is this thought plausible?" If your answer is: "Yes of course it is", you can ask yourself: "Is that really true?" Write down those things that indicate that your thought is *not reasonable*. Then you will see the whole picture and logical inconsistencies better.

You can transfer your reasoning to someone else. If he has the same problem, what advice would you give him?

You can judge your thoughts "using a scale" instead of the all or-nothing-mind-frame. If you make a mistake at work; how serious is it, on a scale from 0 to 10?

Talk to others about your problems. You will discover that most people are worried about making mistakes. If you call yourself "unsuccessful" ask others what they mean by "unsuccessful". Everyone makes mistakes from time to time but that does not mean that they are unsuccessful.

Do not be too dramatic when you talk about your mistake as this will help you to be less emotional about the whole situation. Instead of saying: "I really messed that up" you can say: "I do not like what I did, it was a mistake".

Examine the factors that led to your making the mistake. Admit your part in it but also acknowledge when other factors contributed to your failure.

Feelings of guilt trigger stress reflexes that can catch you even more comprehensively in a vice of a mind trap.

Make a list of the pros and cons of thoughts like: "I know I shall fail"

Be specific: "That mistake I made on Monday after lunch was bad".

In the same way that you negatively badger yourself about everything, thereby leading you to believe that it is all true, you could persistently concentrate on positive facets of yourself especially ones that you know are true. Positive affirmations (validating thoughts) promote good self-esteem.

You can decrease the strength of a mind trap by adding a liberating thought in direct association to the "mind-trap-thought" and then rehearse the liberating thought every time the mind trap reappears; e.g. "now I'm in a mind trap, induced by a stress reflex".

You can work on your thoughts in ways mentioned above, or you can experiment with your stress reflexes. You might need the support of a therapist but you can do a lot by yourself. At the same time as you are exposed to a worrying thought – pay attention to what you feel inside.

Oscillate between these two zones of attention; your worrying thought and the perceptions inside your body. If you experience some aspect of the stress reflex like a sensation in your stomach or muscle tension, focus on those parts of your body and increase that specific sensation. Then reduce the sensation – increase the sensations again – decrease, and so on.

When you experience that you can increase and decrease stress sensations at will you will feel liberated. You are on the road to disconnecting your stress reflexes from the particular thought that has become a mind trap.

In this way, you can, step by step, take control over your stress reflexes and reduce your helplessness.

A worrying thought may be realistic and can be about something that you have to deal with. In that case, it is important that you are relaxed enough to be creative and wise when you search for a solution. You need to be relaxed enough to sleep well so you can regain enough energy to do what you need to do.

But if the thought has become a mind trap, it is essential that you find a way to cope with your stress reflex so it will not dominate your attention, your physical reactions, your feelings, behaviour and self-esteem.

Emotion: Feelings per se are not "wrong" because they only reflect what you think, see or hear.

However, do not let your feelings act *as proof* that your thoughts are true. Even if a feeling makes your thoughts feel right it may be just an expression of the self's habit of feeling guilt, fear or aggression. Guilt, fear and aggression can also affect your behaviour so that what you most fear actually will occur.

The importance of positive thinking is often emphasized in public discussion about mental health as this will lead to positive feelings. This is true because feelings are consequential to thoughts and sensory impressions.

However, there is more to it than that. If you are living in a socially untenable situation, that is abusive and generates anxiety – positive thinking can work as a mind trap. Inside, you feel torn. "It is not too bad – there are lots of people who are much worse off than I am – I should not be complaining".

There is a contradiction in thinking that everything is fine while at the same time feeling totally unhappy. You do not want to be in this situation any more! Simply concentrating on whether thoughts are positive or negative is a far too limited focus.

Should you be worried? Can you access your inherent creativity in these circumstances? Is it reasonable to assume that you bear responsibility for all this or is someone else also accountable for things being the way they are?

Feelings should be respected and examined. What thoughts and impressions have given us these feelings? Feelings can function as guidelines and compasses as we steer our way through life. Where am I? In what direction should I go? Feelings and dreams tell you something about yourself and your relations to others.

I have worked as a psychologist for over fourty years and I sometimes ask myself why I put such emphasis on physical well-being during my sessions with clients, young and old, alike.

Above all, my contact with people who suffer from panic attacks has convinced me of how important physical stress reactions are for mental health. The phenomenon "human" is always made up of both body and soul. Every person has sensory impressions, physiological conditions, a certain behavioural repertoire, mental activity and feelings.

I feel that the importance of the body's (physiological) reactions for mental health has been neglected and put aside in most of the early literature on psychology. Therefore, I think it is important to highlight the client's physical condition and not only concentrate on all the other quandaries in life that preoccupy the client.

In a state of depression the importance of three basic physiological needs becomes evident; sleep, varied diet and physical exercise. If these needs are not met satisfactorily mental problems, such as concentration difficulties, memory impediments, irritation and sooner or later anxiety and depression will ensue.

By diminishing physiological imbalances with effective sleep, varied diet and sufficient exercise, you improve the conditions for dealing with all the other things that lead to stress, anxiety and depression.

Being in a state of mindfulness, letting uncomfortable thoughts exist without fighting against them, is mentally healing. The inner stress can "dissolve" when the body relaxes and breathing becomes calm. Meditation and yoga, liberating dance and relaxation exercises are all good techniques to employ.

The importance of relationships with people and pets for our mental and physical health is evident in scientific research. Mutual care and an open relationship are both factors that reduce psycho-somatic stress. Fight flight reflexes are activated more seldom, and more quickly diminished, when they are understood for what they really are, which is the case in an open, positive relationship.

Self-esteem: What can you do to achieve better selfesteem? Well, self-esteem is rooted in all FRAMES factors. It depends on what impressions you focus on and what thoughts you have about yourself. Filtering focus affects self-esteem just as self-esteem affects filtering focus.

Therefore, it is important to be aware that we function this way psychologically. You can lower your self-esteem by solely focus on negative impressions from within or from the outside world.

Self-esteem is determined by our physical reactions to different situations. You need to learn how to handle your body and its reactions. How do you relax? How do you manage food, exercise and rest? How can you practice mindfulness thereby letting troublesome thoughts go?

Self-esteem is also dependant on the actions you take. How should you act in order to feel content afterwards? It is important not to damage yourself and do things that go against your inner convictions.

Self-esteem is, above all, dependant on how you see yourself and what place you see yourself as having in the world. What is your mental map like? What do you say to yourself?

Chapter 13. At the health care centre

My patients were referred to psychotherapy when they suffered from different anxiety related symptoms.

The first time I meet my client I ask: "What can I do for you"? The answer can be very vague like "Everything" or "I don't know – I feel really bad". The answer can be specific like "I want help with my claustrophobia". In any case I start to sketch the six FRAMES components on the whiteboard relating to their story. I ask probing questions – "What makes you feel bad", "How long have you felt like this?" or "What are your thoughts about your feelings?"

I write down the client's answers on the whiteboard in their respective positions in the FRAMES model. Then I add connecting arrows to illustrate the dynamics of FRAMES' interaction. Connections are often cyclical; "I feel bad when I think of..." and "I start to think of... when I feel bad". Then I investigate how feelings of anxiety, irritation, fear or aggression mutually influence body sensations, or the effect they have on the client's behaviour, thoughts, focus of attention and self-esteem.

In the process, at some point, I start to focus on psycho-educative information about the fight-flight-response and the consequences of prolonged arousal in the body. Clients usually recognize the phenomena described in chapter 5 (Prolonged anguish evoking State of Alert).

Some patients recognize several signs of anxiety while others report only a few – but of course the extent of awareness also varies.

Then we reason about how to do reflex interventions. The strategy involves progressive relaxation, scanning attention through the whole body and helping the client to be aware of functional vs. dysfunctional breathing.

The process of reflex intervention begins with investigation of the client's perception of his/her body sensations that are aroused by worrying thoughts or frightening sensory input (phenomena in outer situations, or phenomena in the body).

In my role as a therapist I pay attention to the client's body language (noting, amongst other things, whether breathing is chest or diaphragm breathing) as well as to the information that has been revealed in the initial FRAMES analysis.

My part of the desensitization process is to coach relaxation and then remind the client of some unpleasant memory from the past or some worrying thoughts about the future – and the client investigates what happens in his/her body when he/she imagines that specific event.

I ask the client: "Do you notice anything happening in your body?"

As the client becomes aware of body sensations I encourage him to willfully increase and then decrease the intensity of the sensations.

Clients are usually surprised and fascinated that this is actually possible, and I affirm even the smallest success of intensity variation.

Often it is easier to increase than to decrease "the volume" of stress sensations, but some clients are so afraid of being afraid that they, in the earlier stages of therapy, do not manage to increase the sensation, but may succeed in decreasing fight-flight symptoms.

Motion muscle (skeletal muscle) activities, like pull a face, lifting the shoulders or chest breathing, are often subconscious. In most instances, sensations of automatic muscle activity are not in the focus of attention.

If we increase and decrease such sensations we become more aware of them. As a bonus we can also become more aware of connections between such muscle activities and worrying thoughts or connections between outer stimuli and such muscle activities.

If the client finds it difficult to decrease sensations, originating from stress reflexes, I encourage him to pay attention to respiration and to "breathe trough" the symptom with calm diaphragm breathing. Calm breathing will calm the whole body, but the relaxation response is often slower than the fight-flight response. The relaxation process can be disrupted by any arousing thought.

Sometimes relaxation is so effective that the client does not experience any stress sensations within the body when I remind him of his worrying thoughts.

We could consider that an unsuccessful exposure in the desensitization therapy work. But, on the other hand, it is progress per se that the client experiences calmness when he is reminded of his worrying thoughts. This situation is also an excellent opportunity to give positive hypnotic suggestions.

Some creative clients who do not succeed in reducing a sensation that arises in a fight-flight response do find ways to change inner focus to some other part of the body and then focus the worrying sensation again – in a new approach – and manage to reduce fight-flight response this way.

One important aspect of body awareness is to notice whether we start to breathe costally when the body is alerted, as this will ultimately lead to hyperventilation and dizziness. If this happens clients usually find a way to reduce hyperventilation in therapy – sometimes with my support – and eventually manage to breathe calmly with the diaphragm in real life situations.

Besides hyperventilation, dizziness and distraction, palpitations are a very common sensation during arousal. It is also possible for clients to increase or decrease palpitations during a therapy session.

In addition, we can link positive memories to palpitations – and come to understand that palpitations are merely the body's response to a stimulus, and that they can be meditate on and not be afraid of them.

Here is a brief report from a "body-mind-session" with a young woman, Julia, who was recently examined for dyslexia; at school they have new promising plans for her education. She has always been appreciated by her school mates, so the school yard and the school building per se do not make her feel bad, but words like examination, class, homework and classroom upset her stomach.

In a session, at my practice, she sits in a leanedback position in an armchair concentrating her attention on her body by relaxation of all skeletal muscles, in due order. First she briefly tenses a muscle group. She then relaxes that muscle group and focuses on that same specific group while it is slowly coming to rest.

When we come to the diaphragm I tell her to be extra focused on the feeling in this specific area of her body, as it automatically tenses and relaxes. The diaphragm is central for conscious relaxation. After relaxation I ask her to scan the whole body and to estimate her arousal on a scale (between 1 to 10).

Then I say the words – examination, class, homework and classroom – and she gets a distinct feeling in her stomach. I ask her to increase that feeling and she does it easily. I commend her and ask her to decrease the feeling by focusing on her diaphragm breathing – activating the relaxation response. She also manages to do that. Then I ask if she can say something to herself in connection to her diminishing stomach reflex, something she later on can use as a trigger for the relaxation response.

After some consideration she answers: "Everything is going to be all right". We repeat the procedure, I repeat the words and she increases the intensity of the feeling in her stomach – and then she reduces the feeling with a combination of diaphragm breathing and saying to herself "Everything is going to be all right".

Through this procedure she differentiates a disturbing body phenomenon (pain in the stomach) related to fight-flight response from an automated mental fixation and from the fightflight conditioned words (examination, class, homework and classroom).

In order to get started in this kind of body-mind discriminating process we can evoke body sensations related to fight-flight by different therapeutic techniques; guided imagery, role play (e.g. gestalt therapy's empty chair technique), talking in the "here and now" ("Do you feel…?" – instead of "Did you feel…?") or by the client's action in real life situations.

There is a therapeutic impact on mind traps when we discover that the mind by itself can influence the body in different ways, and body phenomena can influence the mind in different ways.

One client, a young man, says after a body-mindinvestigation-session: "I didn't realize until now that my face and arms get tense when my thoughts are on Christmas". (Christmas is a catastrophe in his family every year).

A young woman wants my help for her panic attacks. In conversation she reveals that she also suffers from several phobias. She has a characteristic twitch of the shoulders when she tells me about these phobias. After a while I ask her if she has some earlier memories connected to this specific twitch of her shoulders. She breaks down and starts to cry.

She tells me about the sexual abuse she was subjected to when she was a little child. She has never before associated her phobias and anxiety with these early experiences.

It becomes possible for her to process these experiences that she never before talked to anyone about – her fear, disgust, her sleeping difficulties and feelings of shame. That characteristic twitch of the shoulders guides her in the therapeutic process.

Another client, Sam, is an alcoholic who has not used alcohol for nine years. He was addicted to alcohol from the age of sixteen to thirty-one, and was during this time convicted for assault. He now suffers from pain in his back, headache and tinnitus.

He wants help in dealing with his fear of his pent up aggression and his fear of illness.

In a session when his mind is on his mother's impending death he has great difficulties breathing with the diaphragm. I help him to breathe with his stomach by holding my right hand on his stomach, right under his rib cage. Then he manages to breathe with the diaphragm but his chest is tense, warm and shivering. I tell him to take a deep breath and briefly hold his chest in that tense position and then exhale and find relaxation in his chest muscles.

After this session he says that he wants to find out more about his body. He wants to take care of himself. Last but not least he wants to get out of his codependence on his mother's fear and his father's alcoholism and get rid of his obsessive habit of saving friends in distress despite the fact that they do not do the same for him.

In guided imagery, psychodrama or sensory stimulation of any kind, the client may become aware of "forgotten" inner pictures or other memory traces associated with stressful or joyful body sensations. This can make way for analysis of other subconscious psychological matters that are associated with our emotional experiences. Therapy work can be focused on a specific request from the client, but it can also be used to adress many areas of life.

Life is a journey and hopefully we can reveal and process unfinished psychological business (FRAMES experiences which we do not fully comprehend) hurtful memories that contribute to uncertainty and lower selfesteem.

Awareness of all aspects of the here-and-now situation presupposes openness to all components of FRAMES.

But "here-and-now-FRAMES" may be influenced by "where and when? – feelings".

In my experience as a therapist I have become more and more convinced that depression and anxiety can be dealt with by adopting mindfulness – being aware of the present moment. Mindfulness involves calm diaphragm breathing when processing memories, or plans for the future. Worrying thoughts about the future or disturbing memories from the past cannot dominate to the same extent when we are calm. Thoughts are processed and integrated in a greater perspective.

A client wondered why his depression diminishes and he feels so calm every time he leaves my practice. He had been on medication for depression for many years. He said he felt his spirits lifting and his passion for life coming back. He is a scientist and he seeks explanations.

I am convinced that modern techniques for scanning the brain will give us some answers in the future. The other night I watched a programme about Dr Sara W. Lazar, who is a psychologist at Harvard Medical School. She has compared brain scans of a group of experienced meditators with those of a group without meditation experience.

In her study, Lazar found that regular meditation increases the girth of those brain areas associated with cognition, emotional processing and well-being. Why? Is it that people with more substantial neuron structures in these areas are more apt at meditation or is it because new connections are created during meditation?

Maybe reflection while the body is relaxed opens our minds and broadens our awareness thus making way for new associations in the brain and making our whole body-mind-complex more balanced and open-minded – i.e. it puts us in a position opposite that we experience due to inner stress and mind traps.

Reaching a state of awareness – mindfulness – is a matter of attention. It is about focus of attention, attention span, attention flow and awareness of present attention. (What is on my mind right now?).

Attention in people with phobia (or obsessions of any kind) is often directed in some "irrelevant" direction – e.g. the walls in a small room, escape routes, catastrophic thinking and feelings of horror (at claustrophobia), instead of focusing diaphragm breathing, relaxation of skeletal muscles, how to get out of the mind trap ("this is dangerous") and focusing on calm action.

Conclusion

Thinking with an open mind is not always easy, especially if you are burdened with worry and fear. You can fool yourself into believing that; "if I could just fix this or that part of my life, then everything would be fine". Stress reflexes and mind traps ruin things for us.

Therefore, you may need support and therapy to understand how your psyche works as a whole and how you can extract yourself from worry and inner stress; conditions that manifest themselves in states of anxiety, depression, phobias and compulsive thinking. You have to give yourself time for personal development to reach peace of mind. Mindful awareness of the present moment – here and now in all its FRAMES' aspects can lead the way to inner calm.

Worrying thoughts about the future and thoughts about embarrassing events in the past produce body alert. Inner stress causes more than physical problems. It also leads to tunnel vision, selective hearing and dysfunctional behaviour which are often at the root of mental and social problems.

The way to extricate yourself from stress reflexes and mind traps is dependant on your ability to deal with both sides of the psychosomatic vice; both the stress reflexes and the filtered focus that derives from stressinduced mind traps.

Take care of yourself. Respect your value as a human being. If you, due to stress reflexes, have a tendency to dissociate yourself from parts of yourself you feel ashamed of, and cannot accept – reflect on that, and embrace those parts.

Integrate them into your person; your wise, integrated self – instead of rejecting them.

Integrate yourself into personal integrity and understanding of life at higher levels.

Acknowledge your stress and do all you can to find support mentally and socially to keep inner stress at a low level. Inner stress and inner relaxation are both essential in the body-mind systemic circularity.

It is not enough to sleep well but it is definitely an advantage. It is not enough to eat a balanced diet, but it is definitely an advantage. It is not enough to exercise the body, but it is definitely an advantage. Nourish your body with a varied diet, sufficient exercise and ample rest. You'll be living in it all your life!

It is easier to think clearly in your dealings in life when your body is in a state of balance and your breathing is balanced. If you succeed in coping with stress reflexes in your body you can live your social and mental life in a more open and enlightened manner.

References

Beck, Judith S. (1995-05). Cognitive therapy: Basics and beyond. Guilford Publications.

Garpebring, Staffan. (2004). FRAMES en psykologisk rammodell. Nomen Förlag.

Hendricks, G. & Hendricks, K. (1995) Kroppens egen intelligens. Svenska Dagbladet.

Appendix: Balanced FRAMES vs. Anxiety

A life in balance involves harmony between stimulation and recovery.

If we disregard the need for relaxation and recovery or, due to circumstances beyond our control, do not find peace of mind, we may end up being constantly out of balance.

Unbalanced FRAMES may cause anxiety:

F - That I have difficulties in focusing attention. Perception may be distorted by some systematic bias in the way I interpret experiences.

R - That I have difficulties in mobilizing energy for daily life due to energy level being too high or too low for appropriate action.

A - That action is dysfunctional; anxiety-ridden, inhibited, paralyzed, obsessive or manic.

M - That I easily get caught in mind traps

E - Emotional instability, and

S - That my self efficacy and my self-esteem is lowered.

Since our FRAMES influence the circumstances we find ourselves in (outer situation) and vice versa; well-being requires a balance in the synergy between social interaction and internal FRAMES interaction.

Balanced FRAMES in stress means:

F - Attention is focused on the goal

R - Degree of vigilance is properly adjusted to the situation, and the relationship between stimulation and the resultant urge for gratification is balanced by patience and self-restraint

A - Action is focused on and in accordance with personal values/priorities.

M - Mental focus is aimed towards success while maintaining a cautious mental attitude.

E - Emotional satisfaction.

S - Self-confidence is optimized.

However – if an individual experiences severe trauma, inner stress or grave external stressors over a long period of time, without sufficient rest and recovery, he/she may gradually become exhausted and succumb to depression resulting in limited creativity, lack of initiative and openness for life.

Balanced FRAMES in tranquility means:

F - That attention to the outer zone (external phenomena), or to the inner zone (the body), may be focused on any sensation (here and now) not least the sensation of breathing calmly.

R - That the body is relaxed – free from fight-flight response.

A - That action is based on what "I want to..." rather than on what "I must..."

M - That mental associations come and go freely, not getting fixated on some worrying or exciting thought and that awareness may embrace any FRAMES factor.

E - That I am aware of my emotions.

S - That I accept myself

If you want to analyze your reactions in a given situation you can use the table below.

Situation: ....

F	R	A	M	E	S
What/who you focus on?	Reactions in the body?	Your actions?	Thoughts?	Emotions?	Self-esteem in the situation?
	Stress-level?	Consequences?			Who do you want to be in that situation?